Y0-AZH-291

Robert Griffin III

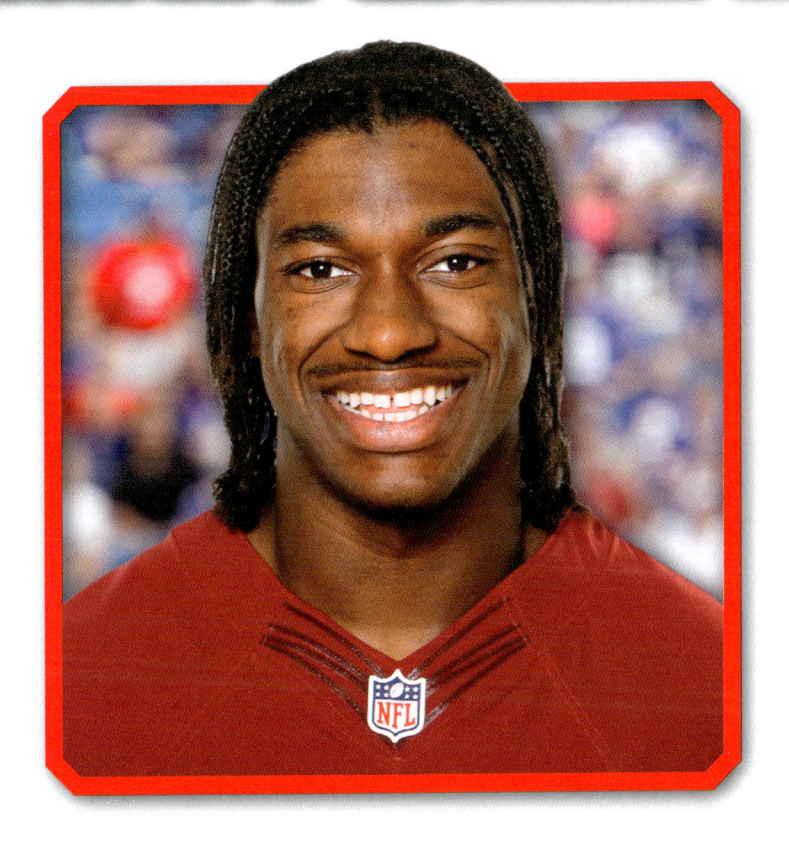

by Nel Yomtov

Consultant: Barry Wilner
AP Football Writer

BEARPORT
PUBLISHING

New York, New York

Credits

Cover and Title Page, © AP Images; 4, © Aaron M. Sprecher/AP Images; 5, © Dan Anderson/ZUMA Press/Newscom; 6, © Aaron M. Sprecher/AP Images; 7, © Robbins Photography; 8, © Jerry Coli/Dreamstime; 9, © Bill Wippert/AP Images; 10, © Steve Traynor/AP Images; 11, © Robbins Photography; 12, © Bingram/Dreamstime; 13, © Robbins Photography; 14, © Craig Ruttle/AP Images; 15, © Helga Esteb/Shutterstock; 16, © Mary Altaffer/AP Images; 17, © Robbins Photography; 18, © Patrick Semansky/AP Images; 19, © Robbins Photography; 20, © Carolyn Kaster/AP Images; 21, © Robbins Photography; 22, © Robbins Photography.

Publisher: Kenn Goin
Editor: Jessica Rudolph
Creative Director: Spencer Brinker
Design: Emily Love
Photo Researcher: Josh Gregory

Library of Congress Cataloging-in-Publication Data

Yomtov, Nelson.
 Robert Griffin III / by Nel Yomtov.
     pages cm. — (Football stars up close)
 Includes bibliographical references and index.
 ISBN-13: 978-1-62724-083-3 (library binding)
 ISBN-10: 1-62724-083-7 (library binding)
 1. Griffin, Robert, III. 1990—Juvenile literature. 2. Football players—United States—Biography—Juvenile literature. 3. Quarterbacks (Football)—United States—Biography—Juvenile literature. I. Title.
 GV939.G775Y66 2014
 796.332'64092—dc23
 [B]
                               2013037789

Copyright © 2014 Bearport Publishing Company, Inc. All rights reserved. No part of this publication may be reproduced in whole or in part, stored in any retrieval system, or transmitted in any form or by any means, electronic, mechanical, photocopying, recording, or otherwise, without written permission from the publisher.

For more information, write to Bearport Publishing Company, Inc., 45 West 21st Street, Suite 3B, New York, New York 10010. Printed in the United States of America.

10 9 8 7 6 5 4 3 2 1

Contents

A Shining Start 4

Early-Season Troubles 6

Like Father, Like Son 8

High School Hero 10

College Superstar 12

Setback and Comeback 14

Rookie Captain 16

Turning Things Around 18

Looking to the Future 20

Robert's Life and Career 22
Glossary 23
Index 24
Bibliography 24
Read More 24
Learn More Online 24

A Shining Start

On September 9, 2012, the Washington Redskins lined up against the New Orleans Saints. It was the first **NFL** game for the Redskins' new **quarterback**, Robert Griffin III. In the first quarter, the Redskins were down 7–3. Robert took the **snap**. The Saints defense charged, but Robert stayed calm. He fired the ball to Redskins **receiver** Pierre Garçon. Pierre caught it and ran into the **end zone**. Robert had thrown his first **touchdown** pass in the NFL!

Robert drops back to throw a pass in the game against the Saints.

From his very first game in the NFL, it was clear that Robert was going to be a star.

Robert's first touchdown pass was 88 yards (80 m) long! It gave the Redskins a 10–7 lead over the Saints.

Early-Season Troubles

In the second quarter, Robert made another touchdown pass. The Redskins ended up beating the Saints 40–32. Redskins fans now had big hopes for a winning 2012–2013 season. However, the Redskins struggled early on. They won only three of their first nine games. Could Robert help the team make a **comeback**?

Robert (right) threw two touchdowns and passed for 320 yards (293 m) against the Saints.

Quarterbacks usually hand off or throw the ball to a receiver. However, because of his speed, Robert often runs the ball down the field himself.

Robert uses his quick moves to avoid being tackled in a 2012 game against the Indianapolis Colts.

Like Father, Like Son

Robert Lee Griffin III was born on February 12, 1990. His parents were living in Japan at the time. The family moved to Texas when Robert was seven years old. Robert's father, Robert Jr., had been a high school basketball and **track** star. He encouraged his son to try many sports, including basketball, baseball, and football. With his father's support, Robert became a great athlete at a young age.

As a child, Robert's favorite football player was John Elway (left), a star quarterback for the Denver Broncos in the 1980s and 1990s.

Robert hugs his mother, Jacqueline, after a 2012 game against the Buffalo Bills.

Robert is close with his family. After Robert joined the Redskins, he asked his parents to move from Texas to the Washington, D.C., area so they could stay close together.

High School Hero

In high school, Robert was a star on the football and track teams. Football was his favorite sport, though. In his junior year, Robert became his school's **starting** quarterback. That season, he passed for more than 2,000 yards (1,829 m) and threw 25 touchdown passes. Robert's amazing speed and accurate passing made him a fan favorite.

Robert Griffin III got the nickname RGIII in high school. The nickname has stuck ever since.

Robert has worn the number ten on his jersey since he was in high school.

On his high school track team, Robert set Texas state records in the 110-meter (120 yd) and 300-meter (328 yd) **hurdles**.

11

College Superstar

Many colleges wanted Robert to play football for them. Robert accepted a **scholarship** to Baylor University in Waco, Texas. He liked that the school had strong football and track teams. The speed and strength Robert showed on the track helped him on the football field. In his freshman year, Robert was chosen as Baylor's starting quarterback. He soon became the team's standout player.

Robert (left) playing for Baylor

NFL teams began to notice Robert as a rising star when he played for Baylor.

Baylor's football team is named the Bears.

Setback and Comeback

Robert had high hopes for his sophomore football season. However, he hurt his knee during a game. Robert sat out most of the season. As he healed, Robert trained hard. He wanted to come back even faster and stronger—and he did! The following season, Robert led Baylor to victory in seven of the team's first nine games. His senior year was even better, with a great 10–3 record.

Robert is sometimes called Superman because his talents seem superhuman. He even wears socks that match this nickname!

In 2012, Robert won the ESPY award for Best Male College Athlete. The ESPYs are awarded each year by ESPN, a sports television network.

In 2011, Robert won the Heisman Trophy. This award is given each year to the best college football player in the country.

Rookie Captain

It was no surprise when the Washington Redskins selected Robert as the second overall pick in the 2012 NFL **draft**. The Redskins' record had been weak the previous season. Despite Robert's efforts, however, the team continued to struggle. The players held a meeting to talk things over. At the meeting, Robert's teammates chose the rookie quarterback to be a team captain! Would this be what the Redskins needed for a turnaround?

Robert (left) was chosen second out of 253 players in the 2012 NFL draft.

Captains work with coaches to solve team problems.

Robert (#10) talks to his coaches and teammates.

Turning Things Around

As a captain, Robert took on a large leadership role. This helped the Redskins win several games in a row. Unfortunately, Robert's knee was injured in a game against the Baltimore Ravens. He was in a lot of pain but still completed two passes while hopping on one foot! In the end, the Redskins won 31–28.

Robert had to miss the next game while he healed. However, he led the Redskins to victory in the two games following his return. Now the team was headed to the **playoffs**.

Robert being helped off the field after his knee was injured

Robert gets ready to take the snap in a game against the Buffalo Bills in 2012.

As a team leader, Robert tried to stay hopeful after getting injured. "I'm feeling the positive vibes," he said. "The fact that we won the game makes everybody feel a lot better."

19

Looking to the Future

In the first game of the 2012–2013 playoffs, the Redskins faced the Seattle Seahawks. In the fourth quarter, Robert fell to the ground when he reached for a snap. His previous knee injury had not fully healed. Robert had to leave the game. Without their leader, the Redskins lost 24–14. The team's season was over. However, Robert promises to return as one of the NFL's best quarterbacks. "I'm going to be the guy that they know will show up every day, every game, every play," he says.

Redskins fans often show their team spirit by wearing Robert's Superman socks.

Robert had surgery to repair his knee after the 2012–2013 season.

In 2013, Robert sold a pair of football shoes he wore during a game for $15,000 to raise money for cancer research.

Robert's Life and Career

★ **February 12, 1990** — Robert Lee Griffin III is born in Okinawa, Japan.

★ **1997** — Robert and his family move to Texas.

★ **2006** — Robert earns a starting quarterback position in high school.

★ **2008** — Robert begins college at Baylor University in Texas.

★ **2010–2011** — In his final year at Baylor, Robert passes for 4,293 yards (3,926 m) and 37 touchdowns.

★ **2011** — Robert is awarded the Heisman Trophy.

★ **2012** — Robert is drafted by the Washington Redskins.

★ **2012** — Robert plays in his first NFL game and helps his team beat the New Orleans Saints 40–32.

★ **2013** — Robert is badly injured in his first playoff game but promises to return the next season.

Glossary

comeback (KUHM-bak) a situation in which a team that is losing quickly scores many points to close the gap

draft (DRAFT) an event in which professional football teams take turns choosing college athletes to play for them

end zone (END ZOHN) the area at either end of a football field where touchdowns are scored

hurdles (HURD-uhlz) a race in which a runner jumps over a series of fence-like objects

NFL (EN-EFF-ELL) letters standing for the National Football League, which includes 32 teams

playoffs (PLAY-awfss) the games held after the end of the regular football season that determine which two teams will compete in the Super Bowl

quarterback (KWOR-tur-bak) a football player who leads the offense, the part of the team that moves the ball forward

receiver (ri-SEE-vur) a football player whose job is to catch a forward pass

scholarship (SKOL-ur-ship) money given to a person so that he or she can go to college

snap (SNAP) the action in which a football is handed to the quarterback, beginning a play

starting (START-ing) being the coach's first choice to play in a game

touchdown (TUHCH-doun) a score of six points that is made by getting the ball across the other team's goal line

track (TRAK) a sport made up of several different running, jumping, and throwing contests

Index

awards 15
Baylor University 12–13, 14
captains 16–17, 18–19
childhood 8
draft 16
high school 10–11
injuries 14, 18–19, 20–21
New Orleans Saints 4–5, 6
parents 8–9
passing 4–5, 6–7, 10, 18
playoffs 18, 20
records 6, 10–11, 14, 16
rookie season 4–5, 6–7, 9, 16, 18–19, 20–21
speed 7, 10, 12
touchdowns 4–5, 6, 10
track 8, 10–11, 12
Washington Redskins 4–5, 6, 9, 16, 18, 20–21

Bibliography

Klemko, Robert. "Robert Griffin III Hurt as Redskins Edge Ravens in OT." *USA Today* (December 9, 2012).

Official Site of the Washington Redskins: www.redskins.com

Read More

Bodden, Valerie. *Robert Griffin III (The Big Time)*. Mankato, MN: Creative Education (2014).

Fishman, Jon M. *Robert Griffin III (Amazing Athletes)*. Minneapolis, MN: Lerner (2013).

Stewart, Mark, and Jason Aikens. *The Washington Redskins (Team Spirit)*. Chicago: Norwood House Press (2008).

Learn More Online

To learn more about Robert Griffin III, visit
www.bearportpublishing.com/FootballStarsUpClose